PECULIAR QUESTIONS

and

PRACTICAL ANSWERS

PECULIAR QUESTIONS

and

PRACTICAL ANSWERS

A LITTLE BOOK OF WHIMSY AND WISDOM

FROM THE FILES OF

THE NEW YORK PUBLIC LIBRARY

ILLUSTRATIONS BY BARRY BLITT

The New York Public Library

St. Martin's Griffin

New York

First published in the United States by St. Martin's Griffin,
an imprint of St. Martin's Publishing Group

PECULIAR QUESTIONS AND PRACTICAL ANSWERS.
Copyright © 2019 by The New York Public Library.
Illustrations copyright © 2019 by Barry Blitt.
All rights reserved. Printed in China.
For information, address St. Martin's Publishing Group,
120 Broadway, New York, NY 10271.

www.stmartins.com

Designed by Devan Norman

Library of Congress Cataloging-in-Publication Data

Names: Blitt, Barry, illustrator. | New York Public Library.
Title: Peculiar questions and practical answers : a little book of
    whimsy and wisdom from the files of the New York Public
    Library / The New York Public Library ; illustrations by
    Barry Blitt.
Description: First edition. | New York : St. Martin's Griffin,
    2019. | Includes bibliographical references.
Identifiers: LCCN 2019022902| ISBN 9781250203625
    (paper over board) | ISBN 9781250203632 (ebook)
Subjects: LCSH: Questions and answers.
Classification: LCC AG195 .P43 2019 | DDC 031.02—dc23
LC record available at https://lccn.loc.gov/2019022902

Our books may be purchased in bulk for promotional,
educational, or business use. Please contact your local bookseller
or the Macmillan Corporate and Premium Sales Department
at 1-800-221-7945, extension 5442, or by email at
MacmillanSpecialMarkets@macmillan.com.

First Edition: October 2019

10   9   8   7   6   5   4   3   2   1

preface

The New York Public Library's mission is to provide free access to information and resources. Generations of students, job seekers, scholars, and a curious public have come to the Library's ninety-two branches, including four research centers across three boroughs (Manhattan, the Bronx, and Staten Island) to access NYPL's vast collections and to take advantage of its librarians' expertise.

The questions posed in this volume are selected from a cache of those written on file cards between the 1940s and the late 1980s, as far as we can tell from the dates on each card. When the staff of the Library discovered them a few years ago in a small gray file box, they inspired awe, laughter, and, most importantly, the box provided a snapshot of the interests of people coming into the Library. Some clearly reflect the times and particular concerns of the day while others could just as well be asked of NYPL—or Google—today.

Since The New York Public Library opened its doors in 1895, its librarians have been greeted with an unending stream of questions. The people of New York City—and beyond—have a voracious appetite for knowledge and, for more than a hundred years, the Library is where they have come for answers. In the 1920s, staff provided instructions on how to shear camels and directed patrons to prints illustrating fourteenth-century corsets. In 1956, a schoolteacher phoned to learn the signatories to the 1888 Suez Treaty. The Library's highly trained staff has even sought an answer to what makes mud stick together.

Providing these answers can be a time-consuming endeavor. To meet growing demand, the Library started the Telephone Reference service in 1968. This later became "Ask NYPL" with email service added in 1996. In September 1999 the Library developed a website that would allow online visitors to, "submit questions to librarians via an online form [and] . . . browse and search through the archive of questions and answers." Ask NYPL staff developed its own question software with Ask Librarians Online, on November 6, 2000.

Currently, the service is administered principally by a dedicated staff of twelve (with modest assistance from librarians throughout NYPL). A chat service is staffed by NYPL librarians Monday through Saturday from 9 a.m. to 6 p.m. These chats are generally brief and the questions asked are usually of a directional or referral nature. In July 2017, the Library transitioned to platforms that allowed the team to also answer questions via Twitter and Facebook.

Despite the myriad ways, online and off, that exist today to search for answers and guidance, the Library's resources are more popular than ever.

CAN YOU GIVE ME THE NAME OF A BOOK THAT DRAMATIZES BEDBUGS?
(1944)

*W*e have not found any books that drama-
tize the lowly bedbug. Bedbugs, though
traumatic to many who encounter them, are rather
undramatic insects. They quietly drink blood, leaving itchy bites on their victims, but are not known to
transmit or spread disease. They are certain to make
one uneasy though. One would like to think that, in
Melville's *Moby-Dick,* Ishmael and Queequeg take
turns harpooning bedbugs, but as we know, they
turned their attention to a certain whale.

DO YOU KNOW HOW I CAN GET A
JOB AS A PEARL DIVER OR A SPONGE
DIVER IN SOUTHERN FLORIDA?
(1945)

As with any job, you need to have the right skills to apply (e.g., know how to swim, and how to coax oysters to cough up pearls) and a good résumé. Connections help as well! While we can't offer swimming or shucking lessons, NYPL's Career Center should be able to help find employers, write a résumé, and make industry connections.

WHAT BOOKS WERE AVAILABLE,
IN 1944, TO A MAN ASKING
FOR BOOKS ON "CHARM FOR MEN"?
(1944)

Since the sixteenth century, men could consult *The Book of the Courtier* by Count Baldassare Castiglione to polish their manners and perfect their charms. For today's aspiring gentleman, perhaps M. Marshall's *Charm School for Guys!: How to Lose the Fugly and Get Some Snugly* (2007) could be of use.

Is it possible to keep an
Octopus in a private home?

IS IT POSSIBLE TO KEEP AN OCTOPUS IN A PRIVATE HOME? (1944)

Yes, but they require a lot of work and you better keep a tight lid on their tank. Octopuses are excellent escape artists. A good place to start your research is The Octopus News Magazine Online (https://www.tonmo.com). Want to learn more about these creatures in general? You can find books about octopuses at your local library under the Dewey number 594.56.

WHAT HORSEPOWER IS REQUIRED TO COVER ALL THE MECHANICAL EQUIPMENT IN WWII?
(1944)

*W*e did not find a source that described in terms of horsepower all energy expended by machinery during the Second World War. One study that we found that may help you calculate a figure is "The Mineral Industry of the British Empire and Foreign Countries, Statistical Summary 1941–1947," published by the Imperial Institute, in 1949. According to this, during the course of the war, the Allied powers produced about 4,581,400,000 metric tons of coal, and the Axis powers about 2,629,900,000, and the Allies about 1,043,000,000 metric tons of crude oil and the Axis about 66,000,000.

We can't say that these resources were all used

for the war effort, but one could look for a baseline number during the years before the war, subtract a reasonable number based on civilian rationing, and then use the remainder to determine how many mineral resources were used. One could then calculate an answer based on those figures, and an average horsepower produced by each resource using machines from that time. You research this at NYPL's General Research Division. We leave the math to you.

HOW many seeds are there in a watermelon?
(1944)

*N*aturally, the exact answer depends on the exact specimen of *Citrullus lanatus* (watermelon), but sources we found state that there are 250–750 seeds in the average American watermelon. Generally the bigger the melon the more seeds there are. Seeds come in many colors, black, red, white (these are developing seeds). Some recent varieties of watermelon are seedless. Which is a shame since there's great nutritional value in the seeds according to sources such as *Foods and Food Production Encyclopedia* by Douglas M. Considine. And don't be worried if you swallow a few. Our stomach acids ensure you will not be growing a watermelon in your stomach.

WHAT IS THE SIGNIFICANCE OF THE HIP MOVEMENT IN THE HAWAIIAN DANCE?
(1944)

*I*t's complicated, depending greatly on the specific movement and the context in which it is placed given that the Hawaiian hula is a sacred ritual dance in which every movement of the performer is codified and deeply symbolic. As definitive a book as it gets is Mahealani Uchiyama's 2016 *The Haumana Hula Handbook for Students of Hawaiian Dance,* which describes in depth the origins, language, etiquette, ceremonies, and the spiritual culture of hula. Ultimately though, the full significance could never be communicated in writing—to paraphrase the famed apothegm, writing about hip movements is like singing about architecture.

When one travels west in the U.S. and crosses the desert, does one cross on camels?

WHEN ONE TRAVELS WEST IN THE U.S. AND CROSSES THE DESERT, DOES ONE CROSS ON CAMELS?
(1946)

*I*f the United States Army had their way perhaps. According to an entry in *The New Encyclopedia of the American West* in 1855 the U.S. Army held about seventy-five camels at Camp Verde, Texas. Secretary of War Jefferson Davis thought they would serve as good pack trains and he was right. The experiment however did not gain much popularity and by the time the Civil War began the project was abandoned. Want to read more on the topic? NYPL has the following in our collection: *Three Caravans to Yuma: The Untold Story of Bactrian Camels in Western America*, by Harlan D. Fowler.

WHICH IS correct: "THE CONSTITUTION OF THE UNITED STATES" or "THE UNITED STATES CONSTITUTION"? (1944)

*A*ccording to the huge and reliable OCLC WorldCat catalog of all printed materials, "The Constitution of the United States of America" has been the official title of editions dating back to 1790. The National Archives, which hosts the original, concurs that this is the official title. If you want it straight from the horse's mouth so to speak, the preamble itself states: "We the People of the United States, in Order to form a more perfect Union, establish Justice, insure domestic Tranquility, provide for the common defence, promote the general Welfare, and secure the Blessings of Liberty to ourselves and our Posterity, do ordain and establish this Constitution for the United

States of America." Hmm. Tricky preposition . . . double-checking the document, we find that it calls on the president to swear into office by saying he will "defend the Constitution of the United States." Phew.

WHAT IS THE PSYCHOLOGICAL
EFFECT OF A BIRTHMARK
ON A CHILD?
(1944)

*W*hat is a birthmark? According to Kids
health.org, newborns often have tempo-
rary pimples or blotches that disappear soon
after they are born. It's also quite common to see
birthmarks on their skin at birth or shortly after.
Birthmarks range from hardly noticeable to dis-
figuring, but no matter how large or small they
are, they can be upsetting. Birthmarks can be flat or
raised, have regular or irregular borders, and have
different shades of coloring from brown, tan, black,
or pale blue to pink, red, or purple. They're mostly
harmless and many even go away on their own or
shrink over time. Sometimes birthmarks are associated with other health problems, though, so we

recommend that you talk with your doctor about whether this might be the case for your child.

How do we help children deal with birthmarks? It can be a shock at first to see a birthmark on your newborn. Nobody is perfect, yet many people have an image of a perfect baby in their heads. If the birthmark is clearly visible, people might ask questions or stare, which can feel rude. It helps to have a simple explanation ready to handle intrusions like this. Most people mean no harm, but it's also okay to let them know if they've gone too far. Even at a young age, kids watch how their parents respond to situations like this. This is where they learn how to cope with others' reactions. Talking simply and openly about a birthmark with kids makes them more likely to accept one as just another part of themselves, like hair color, and to practice simple answers they can use when asked about it: "It's just a birthmark. I was born with it." It's also important emotionally for kids to be around supportive family and friends who treat them normally.

HOW MUCH WOULD IT COST TO FEED AN INFANT FOR ABOUT SIX MONTHS? (1945) WHAT IS THE COST IN 2018?

*N*aturally, the costs of feeding an infant can vary greatly depending on whether they are being nursed by their mother, or being given formula (and then on which formula you use, brand name, generic, etc.). It is difficult to calculate the costs for 1945 but one might be able to dig deep into research on the historical costs of baby formula and cleaning supplies (for the bottles) at NYPL's Science, Industry and Business Library, which keeps materials and records on the cost of living. According to romper.com (June 16, 2018), the typical cost of baby formula is about $165 per month or about $990 for six months.

WHAT COLLEGES GIVE A COURSE FOR TRAINING CHURCH USHERS?
(1945)

*B*ecoming a church usher is often considered a sacred duty, but it is not one that requires formal training. In the classic book *A Guide to Church Ushering* by Homer Elford, Mr. Elford goes over what skills a church usher must possess and the most important is that "the church usher share with the minister an absolute devotion to Christ." So devotion, not college credits, will get you in the door! If you desire instruction on tasks, this is usually handed down from the head usher who would be guided by the minister of the respective church. If you want some modern information on usher practices, you can reach out to an association like the National United Church Ushers Association of America, Inc. They have chapters throughout the country and they provide a "School of Ushering Manual" that provides standards on usher tasks, behaviors, and expectations.

What time does a bluebird sing?

WHAT TIME DOES A
BLUEBIRD SING? (1944)

*W*ell, the eastern bluebird sings whenever it is motivated to. Most often, males are motivated by seeing nice female bluebirds they want to court, or seeing them laying eggs (at which time they sing softly, which is sweet). Females are motivated to sing more rarely, but may do so when they see predators.

You can hear their recorded song at the website of the Cornell Lab of Ornithology and learn more through Vassar College's page as well.

IS IT PROPER TO GO ALONE TO RENO TO GET A DIVORCE?
(1945)

*I*n 1931, Reno reduced its six-month residency requirement for divorces to six weeks. Ranches catered to the trade in what were often referred to as "Reno-vations." By 1946, there were nineteen thousand Reno divorces, a big business that brought in the equivalent of $50 million annually from divorcées as the "ranches" catered to (mostly) women who stayed about six weeks. There was no stigma associated with a woman going alone to one of these ranches, although she'd have plenty of company (cowboys included) milling about. Today, one no longer need to travel to Reno for a divorce. They are widely available across all fifty states.

WHAT IS THE SOCIAL SIGNIFICANCE OF A PERSON PLAYING BLIND MAN'S BLUFF? (1945)

*I*n the book *Game Play: Therapeutic Use of Childhood Games,* a good overview is given on the origin of game playing. Games of all kinds, especially those of a historic nature, usually evolved from spiritual beliefs and rituals. Blind man's bluff, which originated in ancient Greece around 1000 BC, is no different. The game was based on prehistoric rites of human sacrifice. At that time it was called munida or brazen fly. Primarily played by boys, in the game one boy would be blindfolded while the others beat him with papyrus husks.

The game regained popularity during the Elizabethan era in England retaining its roots in ritual behavior but replacing the husks with knotted rope.

As times had changed so did the players of the game. Played by both genders, blind man's bluff became notorious when hitting turned into fondling among the adults who played and it became a favorite game for foreplay among people in the English court. This was ceremoniously ended with the dawning of the stricter Victorian era.

IS THERE A SCHOOL FOR AUCTIONEERS? (1945)

Yes, and you have your choice; check out http://www.auctioneers.org/schools/. Do I have a bid for . . . ?!

WHAT IS THE DIFFERENCE BETWEEN "PIG" AND "PORK"?
(1945)

*P*er *Lobel's Meat Bible*, pig is the beast that squeals just before it is butchered to become pork.

DID ABRAHAM LINCOLN GO TO HARVARD? (1946)

*A*braham Lincoln did not attend Harvard nor in fact any other college or university. Indeed, he may not have had as much as one year of formal education. However, Lincoln's program of reading and self-education may serve as a lesson to all of us. Before he was twenty-one, Lincoln read the King James Bible, Aesop's Fables, John Bunyan's *The Pilgrim's Progress*, Defoe's *Robinson Crusoe*, Parson Weems's *The Life of Washington*, and *The Autobiography of Benjamin Franklin* as well as histories, newspapers, and "everything he could get his hands on." Many of his neighbors and family thought the young Lincoln was lazy for all his "reading, scribbling, writing, ciphering and writing poetry." Lincoln would also read Shakespeare throughout his life.

Did Abraham Lincoln
go to Harvard?

In his time, one did not need to attend law school to become an attorney in Illinois. So, Lincoln also taught himself the law by reading Blackstone's *Commentaries on the Laws of England* and other law books. Of his legal learning, Lincoln stated: "I studied with nobody." Although he never attended any university, Lincoln's speeches, letters, and writings appear in countless anthologies of the best American literature and his influence on American history is enormous.

I RECEIVED A LETTER FROM A
FRIEND IN THE SOUTH SEAS WHO
SAYS HE IS IN A COUNTRY WHERE
MONKEYS HAVE NO TAILS.
WHERE IS HE?
(1945)

*T*he *Simon & Schuster Encyclopedia of Animals* states that there is only one species of monkey that does not have a tail and that is the Barbary macaque. They can be found in Morocco and Algeria. Since your friend was not in that part of the world he likely saw an ape. Apes do not have tails but because they are primates as well and have similarities to monkeys, the two often get confused. There are no monkeys or apes native to the South Seas.

The closest to that area is the gibbon, which is an ape that is found in Southeast Asian countries as well as Java, Borneo, and Sumatra. They are similar in size to a monkey and share common features. This along with their location indicate this is likely the primate your friend came across. Since gibbons can be found in several places within that region, he could have been in any of the aforementioned countries.

HOW DO I PUT UP WALLPAPER?
(1945)

*I*t was probably far more difficult to put up wallpaper in 1945 than it is today. These days you can find many online video tutorials on websites like thisoldhouse.com and hgtv.com. You can find books on this topic at your local library under the Dewey number 698. Some titles that we found in the catalog are: "Professional tips for easy wallpapering" [videodisc] (Westlake Village, CA: Silvermine Video, 2008); *The Complete Guide to Painting & Decorating: Using Paint, Stain & Wallpaper in Home Decor*, revised & updated (Chanhassen, Minn: Creative Pub. Int'l, 2006); and *Creative Wallpaper: Ideas & Projects for Walls, Furniture & Home Accessories* (New York: Lark Books, 2003).

WHO WROTE THE PRAYER THAT
WAS PRESIDENT ROOSEVELT'S
FAVORITE? IT BEGINS WITH
"GOD OF THE FREE,
WE PLEDGE OUR LIVES."
(1945)

*T*he "Prayer for United Nations" was written by the American poet and author Stephen Vincent Benét. The prayer was read to a national radio audience after FDR's death on April 12, 1945, by the actor Raymond Massey who portrayed Lincoln in the Hollywood film: *Abe Lincoln in Illinois*. President Roosevelt had earlier read this same prayer to the nation in a radio address from the White House on Flag Day, June 14, 1942.

HOW MUCH DID NAPOLEON'S BRAIN WEIGH? (1945)

*U*nfortunately, Napoleon's brain was never weighed after his death on St. Helena in 1821. In the nineteenth century there was a belief that the size of a person's brain had a correlation with one's intelligence, and there were a great number of estimates and speculation as to the weight of Napoleon's brain. However, French officials refused the request of one of Napoleon's physicians at the autopsy to open Napoleon's head surgically and it was left intact—although almost bald from the amount of hair Napoleon had sent to his family and friends as mementos.

MAY A FUNERAL BE HELD ON JULY 4TH?
(1945)

A copy of *The High Cost of Dying* by Ruth Mulvey Harmer should provide a reasonable answer, but the internet might provide something more immediate: https://www.imortuary .com/blog/can-i-hold-a-funeral-on-a-holiday/.

At what time is "high noon"?

AT WHAT TIME IS "HIGH NOON"?
(1947)

*A*ccording to the *Oxford English Dictionary* database high noon is defined as midday, so 12:00 p.m.

WHAT IS THE OPPOSITE OF
"A STIFF BEARD"? (1945)

*I*t depends on how you define "opposite." One might say "clean shaven" is diametrically opposed to a stiff beard. But if you want whiskers, then men's periodical *GQ* uses the terms "soft" and/or "supple"—and provides helpful tips to loosen up even the most bristly of beards: https://www.gq.com/story/how-to-grow-a-beard-for-the-first-time.

WHEN WRITING TO A SAILOR,
SHOULD ONE ALWAYS SPELL
THE WORD "WEIGH" AS IN
"ANCHORS AWEIGH" OUT OF
COURTESY, EVEN WHEN IT IS
USUALLY SPELLED "WAY"?
(1945)

*W*hile the Library carries books on etiquette (Emily Post, Amy Vanderbilt, Judith Martin, aka, Miss Manners, etc.), and books on the ways and manners of mariners (*To Swear Like a Sailor: Maritime Culture in America, 1750–1850*, by Paul A. Gilje, 2016), we don't see any sources that describe what, if any, special conventions should be adhered to when corresponding with a sailor and using the word "way." If you are a scrimshaw enthusiast, you could send a message on that or you could just enclose your message in corked bottle because any "weigh" you do it should be fine.

WHAT DOES IT MEAN WHEN YOU'RE BEING CHASED BY AN ELEPHANT?
(1947)

We are going to assume this is a dream and, unless you correct us, we will continue assuming so as we do not wish to even contemplate what it would mean to be chased by an animal thirty times our size with size 40 (U.S.) feet. Since elephants represent power, strength, and intellect and you are being chased, in effect, by these qualities—why are you running? Let the power overtake you, seize the intellect, and embrace your inner strength next time you are asleep. And please don't even ask what it means to be chased by a peacock.

It could also mean you are in very big trouble! But seriously . . . according to *The Amboseli*

What does it mean when you're being chased by an elephant?

Elephants by Joyce Poole and Petter Granli, elephants have been known to lunge, rush at, or pursue another elephant, predator, or other adversary as an act of escalated aggression, sometimes chasing for several kilometers. Males, particularly in musth (mating season), rush at one another and attempt to gore each other with their tusks to show strength and win mates. Chasing can also be part of play behavior in a herd of elephants.

DO YOU HAVE A LIST OF HISTORICAL CHARACTERS WHO WERE AT THE RIGHT PLACE AT THE RIGHT TIME?
(1946)

The Library does not keep such a list. If one existed, it would be pretty subjective. Jesus? Mohammed? Cleopatra? Henry VIII? Madame Curie? Andrew Carnegie? Indeed, these might all be examples of people who were in the right place at the right time. We are not sure that such a list exists elsewhere, but we do believe that such a list could go on and on and on. . . .

WHAT DID A PENNY WEIGH IN 1946?
IN 2018?
(1946)

*T*he Lincoln Shield Cent, which came into circulation in 2010 and is still being produced now in 2018, weighs 2.50 grams (per the U.S. Mint's website, which is full of information you didn't know you needed to know, such as the 1974 plea by Mrs. Mary Brooks, director of the Mint, for people to return the 30 billion pennies she speculates are hiding "in shoeboxes and pickle jars").

The Lincoln Wheat Cent from 1946 weighs 3.11 grams—if you're wondering why: it was 95 percent copper then and only 2.5 percent copper now.

CAN YOU GIVE ME THE BIRTH AND DEATH DATES OF FIFTY FAMOUS WOMEN?
(1946)

*H*ere are a dozen to get you started:

* Sappho, born 630 BC, died 570 BC
* Cleopatra (Cleopatra VII Philopator), born 69 BC, died August 10 or 12, 30 BC
* Mary Wollstonecraft Shelley, born August 30, 1797, died February 1, 1851
* Marie Skłodowska Curie, born November 7, 1867, died July 4, 1934
* Amelia Earhart, born July 24, 1897, disappeared July 2, 1937
* Marian Anderson, born February 27, 1897, died April 8, 1993

* Queen Victoria, born May 24, 1819, died January 22, 1901
* Helen Keller, born June 27, 1880, died June 1, 1968
* Mother Teresa, born August 26, 1910, died September 5, 1997
* J. K. Rowling, born July 31, 1965 (living)
* Sonia Sotomayor, born June 25, 1954 (living)
* Beyoncé Giselle Knowles-Carter, born September 4, 1981 (living)

HOW MANY NEUROTIC PEOPLE ARE THERE IN THE U.S.?
(1946)

*I*t is impossible to answer this question with any real accuracy. Though neurosis was eliminated from the *Diagnostic and Statistical Manual of Mental Disorders* in 1994 (*New York Times,* March 12, 2012, "Where Have All the Neurotics Gone?" by Benedict Carey), it is still used to describe a class of functional mental disorders involving chronic anxiety (panic disorder, social anxiety, obsessive-compulsive disorder). The diagnosis appears to have enjoyed favor when Freud and psychoanalysis held more sway in American culture, and results from questionnaires that determine neuroses haven't changed much in adults since the 1950s. Neuroticism among college students, on the other hand, appears to have increased, by as much as 20 percent. But being neurotic isn't all that bad. Neurotics tend to be intelligent and creative, obsessively working out solutions. A recent study (July 2017, "When Is Higher Neuroticism Protective Against Death?" by Gale, Čukić, Batty, et al. University of Edinburgh) has shown that certain types of neuroticism may be linked with a longer life as neurotics tend to seek medical advice more that the average person.

CAN YOU GIVE ME THE NAME OF ANY AMERICAN INDIAN GOD OF SPECIOUS THINKING?
(1946)

As "specious" means superficially plausible, but actually wrong or misleading in appearance, there may be a few trickster figures and deities among the Native American mythologies that fit that description. The coyote, in some Navajo legends, is a cunning figure, but contains both good and evil and pushes the boundaries of behavior. The raven, in Northwest coastal myth, cleverly deceives others in his quest for food, but also is responsible for profound changes to the world.

can mice throw up?
(1949)

A study titled "Why Can't Rodents Vomit? A Comparative Behavioral, Anatomical, and Physiological Study," published in 2013 in PLOS One, concluded that they cannot and that "absent brainstem neurological component is the most likely cause." Their brains are just not wired for this action.

Can mice throw up?

IS PALESTINE A CITY IN JERUSALEM OR IS JERUSALEM A CITY IN PALESTINE?
(1947)

*S*ources we consulted, including *The Columbia Gazetteer of the World*, *The World Book Encyclopaedia*, and *the Encyclopædia Britannica* describe Palestine as a region in the Middle East at the eastern end of the Mediterranean Sea, and Jerusalem as a city in the Middle East. Control of the Palestine region has changed many times over the centuries. Jerusalem is currently the capital city of Israel and is considered the world's largest holy city.

WHERE CAN I BUY A CHAMELEON?
(1947)

A chameleon is considered an exotic pet. According to *Reptiles* magazine a breeder, someone who specializes in breeding animals, reptiles and the like, would be the best resource for buying an exotic pet and the best resource for learning how to care for one. *Reptiles* magazine offers a list of local herpetological societies that should be able to help you find a reputable seller or breeder (since importation of most reptiles in to the United States is strictly controlled). See http://www.reptilesmagazine.com/Reptile- Community/Reptile-Clubs/. You can also check in with a veterinarian office that specializes in reptiles or you might look online for reptile expos such as the National Reptile Breeders' Expo that occurs annually.

WHAT IS THE THERAPEUTIC VALUE OF ESSENCE OF PINE NEEDLES?
(1947)

*P*ine needle tea is rich in vitamin C (five times what is found in lemons), antioxidants, and can be used as an expectorant for coughs and chest congestion. The tea is also believed to help one live longer and can help treat depression, allergies, and high blood pressure. Pine needles also smell nice.

WHAT IS THE EYE COLOR OF A SILVER FOX? (1947)

Silver foxes can have brown eyes, hazel eyes, orange eyes, yellow eyes and—in captivity— even blue eyes. This is because the "silver fox" is exactly the same species as the red fox, only it has been bred to have a darker fur color. As it has been a fashionable form of apparel for many decades, a "silver fox" is usually the result of selective breeding by the fur industry into exactly the right shade of pelt that will appeal to those who buy it. It is distinct from the gray fox which is an entirely different species from the red fox and is predominant in the Pacific states. It was never bred as the "silver fox" and the gray fox also has more than one eye color.

WHaT KIND OF aPPLe
DID eVe eaT?
(1956)

*T*he Bible fails to identify the varietal type of fruit, noting only that it was "seeded." (It is depicted as a pomegranate and not an apple in all early representations.) The actual type of apple, however, is irrelevant to understanding the parable. The fruit symbolized the knowledge of good and evil. In this librarian's opinion, that sounds sinfully delicious.

What kind of apple
did Eve eat?

CAN I GET A BOOK TELLING ME HOW TO BE THE MISTRESS OF CEREMONIES AT A MUSICAL ORGY?
(1948)

*I*f by "musical orgy" you mean a gathering where you and others listen to lots and lots of music (where "orgy" is defined as an "excessive indulgence in a specified activity") then NYPL does have books on MC-ing, such as April Calthorpe's 1957 classic *How to Be a Master of Ceremonies* and the more contemporary *Rap and Hip Hop Culture* by Fernando Orejuela (2014). If you have another definition of "orgy," then we don't see any "how-to-throw-an-orgy" manuals in our collection, but you could look through Henry Spencer Ashbee's copy of *The Encyclopedia of Erotic Literature: Being Notes Bio-, Biblio-, Icono-Graphical and Critical, on Curious and Uncommon Books* by Pisanus Fraxi (1962).

WHAT IS THE LIFE CYCLE OF AN EYEBROW HAIR? (1948)

*T*here are three phases in the life of an eyebrow hair: Anagen (growth), Catagen (resting or intermediate), and Telogen (shedding) with the average life span being about four months. According to the Bosley Hair Transplant Company, the average person has 250 to 500 hairs per eyebrow. The older you get, the longer it takes to grow eyebrow hair.

WHERE CAN I GET ALL THE AVAILABLE STATISTICS ON VOLUME OF BUSINESS, MONEY INVOLVED, ETC. IN THE SALE OF CADAVERS? (1948)

*T*his article might be a little stiff, but . . . https://www.reuters.com/investigates /special-report/usa-bodies-brokers says, "As with other commodities, prices for bodies and body parts fluctuate with market conditions. Generally, a broker can sell a donated human body for about $3,000 to $5,000, though prices sometime top $10,000. But a broker will typically divide a cadaver into six parts to meet customer needs. Internal documents from seven brokers show a range of prices for body parts: $3,575 for a torso with legs; $500 for a head; $350 for a foot; $300 for a spine. . . ."

can you make a toast with water? (1948)

*T*oasting superstitions still support the idea that toasting with water is akin to wishing bad luck or even death upon a person. We have the ancient Greeks to thank for this as they toasted their departed loved ones with glasses of water. It was an homage to the River Lethe, upon which the deceased sailed to the Underworld. Toasting etiquette, however, is continually evolving and varies from country to country. While some etiquette mavens say that it is fine to toast with water, others say that it is a big no-no. In the end, you really need to know your audience. For more information check out "Modern Etiquette: Guidelines for Giving Toasts" (*Lifestyle*, October 22, 2012) or "Toasting Etiquette: Do's and Don'ts" (*HuffPost*, December 31, 2013).

WHY IS THE PACIFIC OCEAN AT A DIFFERENT LEVEL FROM THE ATLANTIC?
(1949)

*A*ccording to the 2000 book *What Einstein Told His Barber: More Scientific Answers to Everyday Questions* by Robert L. Wolke, the seas of the world all have the same average level ("mean sea level"), however there are factors including wind, tides, coastline geography, salinity, and gravity that create long-term variations from place to place. For instance, the difference between the tides on the Atlantic side of the Panama Canal are around two feet, whereas high and low tide levels on the Pacific side are as much as 28 feet apart, but the average levels between Atlantic and Pacific sides is more or less equal. (They have been found to be about 8 inches different, which is pretty close to equal, and is due to factors including currents, differences in water density due to salinity and temperature, and other factors that only an oceanographer could explain). The depths of the two bodies of water are different as well. The Atlantic Ocean reaches depths of up to 13,000 feet while the Pacific Ocean extends to depths of up to 35,000 feet. These factors along with erosion on the ocean floor, which has caused submarine canyons and channels to form in various spots, are why the two oceans are at different levels. According to NASA Science (science.nasa .gov/earth-science/oceanography), oceans exist at the same mean sea levels, but tides and currents contribute to the dynamic topography of all ocean surfaces.

I've heard that Roquefort cheese is fermented by worms, and I'd like to concur on that.

I'VE HEARD THAT ROQUEFORT
CHEESE IS FERMENTED BY WORMS,
AND I'D LIKE TO CONCUR ON THAT.
WOULD YOU CONCUR?
(1960)

*T*he Stinky Cheese Man and I do not con-cur. *Penicillium roqueforti* mold is used in the creation of this cheese. Sadly, our earthbound friends have nothing to do with it. If you need some cheesy inspiration, check out the "How It's Made: Roquefort Cheese" video from the "How It's Made" channel on YouTube.

HOW DO YOU PRONOUNCE "SIUOL"? IT'S "LOUIS" SPELLED BACKWARDS AND I'M USING IT IN A NOVEL I'M WRITING.

(1949)

According to librarian Barbara Thomas at the Graduate School of Applied Linguistics, "Rules of pronunciation are that if a syllable is open (ending in a vowel), it is pronounced as a long vowel. Siuol would be divided into three syllables: si / u / ol. The first two syllables would be long and the last short, since it is followed by a consonant. So the pronunciation would sound like see'-oo-əl with the accent on the first syllable and the final syllable being more like the schwa of an unaccented, short vowel."

May we suggest something? You're the author, of course, but perhaps you might consider a simpler name for your character? Like Fred? Fred's a good name.

WHERE CAN YOU GET A DOCTOR OF DIVINITY DEGREE BY CORRESPONDENCE?
(1949)

*D*id you perhaps mean Master of Divinity? Doctor of Divinity, as we found out, is an honorary degree. We reached out to the Association of Theological Schools Commission on Accrediting and the commission does not approve degrees offered by correspondence. But there are schools that offer distance learning. To search for programs, please visit ats.edu.

DO YOU HAVE ANY BOOKS ON THE SCIENCE OF ATHAR, WHICH IS THE SCIENCE OF DEDUCING INFORMATION FROM CAMEL TRACKS?
(1949)

*A*las, we do not find any books specifically on Athar, even outside of NYPL, as it is a very obscure practice; NYPL's collection includes books on tracking (*Crinkleroot's Book of Animal Tracking* by Jim Arnosky, 1979), navigation methods (*The Natural Navigator: A Watchful Explorer's Guide to a Nearly Forgotten Skill* by Tristan Gooley, 2012), camels (*Cumin, Camels, and Caravans: A Spice Odyssey* by Gary Paul Nabhan, 2014), and the Bedouin and other peoples of the desert (*The Last of the Bedu: In Search of the Myth* by Michael Asher, 1996). The most we found comes from the 1858

Annual Report of the Secretary of War, in which is found a detailed letter by one W. Re Kyan Bey on the "Treatment and Use of the Dromedary," including a page on tracking camels.

Athar was associated with the Bedouin tribe, a nomadic group of Arabs that inhabit the deserts of the Middle East and North Africa. In his book *Arabia: The Cradle of Islam* (published in 1900), scholar S. M. Zwemer says, "the camel's foot leaves data for the Bedouin science of Athar—the art of navigation for the ship of the desert." Since it is not recognized as an official "science," further research would require learning more about the Bedouin tribes practices. Some possible titles include: *Culture Change in a Bedouin Tribe: The ʿarab al-Ḥǧerāt, Lower Galilee, A.D. 1790–1977* by Rohn Eloul or *Bedouin Life in the Egyptian Wilderness* by Joseph J. Hobbs.

IF a POISONOUS snake BITES
ITSELF, WILL IT DIE?
(1949)

*T*he "Are Snakes Susceptible to Their Own Venoms?" article on the The Naked Scientists website states that venomous snakes can be susceptible to their own venom. Some snakes, however, have been found to have antivenom in their system that protects them. If a snake happens to swallow some of its own venom it will be fine. Venom is made of protein and it will break down when it gets into the digestive juices in the stomach. Just a little something to wrap your mind around.

WHERE IN NEW YORK CAN YOU BUY BULLETPROOF VESTS?
(1950)

*T*hese days, bulletproof jackets and vests can be bought online. Many are made of Du-Pont's Kevlar fabric and offer varying degrees of protection from ballistic, stab, and spike attacks, in both overt and covert styles. During WWII and the Korean War, body armor made of ballistic nylon was developed that provided some protection from ammunition fragments but was not effective against most rifle and pistol fire. It was not until the 1960s that new fibers were discovered that were truly bullet resistant (bulletsafe.com).

IN WHAT OCCUPATIONS MAY ONE BE BAREFOOTED? (N.D.)

*P*igéage/grape stomping, hand modeling, fire-walking, lifeguard, to name but a few.

In what occupations may one
be barefooted?

can you tell me the relationship between taxes and medieval music?

(1949)

*H*ave you ever heard a Gregorian chant? Its composition and performance had to be paid for.

Taxes in medieval times were collected in the form of currency, in agricultural produce, and in goods and services provided through the land-tenure system by which they flowed to the Crown, the nobility and landed gentry, and to the Catholic Church. Historians of medieval music usually distinguish between ecclesiastical music, designed for use in church or in religious ceremonies, and secular music for use in royal and baronial courts, celebrations of certain religious events, and public and private entertainments of the people.

As literacy, and musical notation in particular, were largely confined to the clergy in this period, much more church music than secular music survives. However, the composition and performance of medieval music at church and court was paid for with what would today be considered taxes.

WHEN, BEFORE 1866, WAS THERE NO FULL MOON IN FEBRUARY?
(1950)

*T*he *Journal of the British Astronomical Association* (vol. 30, 1920) offers the calculations of a Mr. S. H. Gaythorpe, who used the syzygy tables in De Morgan's *Book of Almanacs* to compute which years February had no full moon. To answer your questions, he (and other sources) give the year of 1847. The general pattern is every nineteen years, but it does depend, owing to what noted astronomer W. Shakespeare described as the moon's inconstant nature.

WHAT KIND OF GLASS SHOULD I PUT IN MY GREENHOUSE IN CUBA?
(1950)

A search in our catalog for greenhouses—design and construction—brings up two titles that might aid you with your research: *The Complete Guide to Greenhouses & Garden Projects* (Cool Springs Press, 2011) and Ortho's *All About Greenhouses* (Des Moines, Iowa: Meredith Books, 2001).

You might also want to reach out to the New York Botanical Garden Mertz Library to see what additional resources they may have to best answer your question.

What did women use for shopping bags before paper bags came into use?

WHAT DID WOMEN USE FOR SHOPPING BAGS BEFORE PAPER BAGS CAME INTO USE?
(N.D.)

*T*he paper bag was invented in 1852, the handled shopping bag in 1912. Plastic shopping bags rose to prominence in the 1960s before achieving worldwide shopping domination by the early 1980s. Prior to the common use of a common bag, women—and men for that matter—used their hands and arms and any other vessel at their disposal to carry as much as they possibly could. The paper bag was actually invented so that shoppers could purchase more at one time!

WHO WERE THE MAKERS OF
THE INK USED TO SIGN THE
DECLARATION OF INDEPENDENCE?
(1946)

*T*imothy Matlack (1730–1829, Secretary of Pennsylvania during the American Revolution), was chosen to engross (transcribe) the original Declaration of Independence in July 1776. According to the National Archives website (archives.gov), the Declaration was written on parchment with iron gall ink. "Iron gall ink, the kind typically used in Matlack's day, included tannic acid (from oak galls), iron (from nails or iron scraps), a binder (often gum Arabic), and sometimes a colorant. Light in color when it was applied, the ink darkened as it oxidized to an intense purplish black. Over time, iron gall inks age to a warm brown." We were unable to ascertain information on the manufacturer.

WHAT IS THE POEM ON THE BASE
OF THE STATUE OF LIBERTY?
(1950)

According to the Poetry Foundation, the lines engraved on the pedestal of the Statue of Liberty (in 1903) are from the 1883 sonnet "The New Colossus" by Emma Lazarus, commemorating the plight of immigrants.

DO YOU HAVE A LIST OF FAMOUS MEN WHO WERE BORN PREMATURELY?
(1950)

*T*o name a few (according to the Neonatal Trust):

1. Stevie Wonder
2. Wayde van Niekirk
3. Sir Isaac Newton
4. Samuel Clemens, also known as Mark Twain
5. Sir Winston Churchill
6. Albert Einstein
7. Charles Darwin
8. Napoleon Bonaparte
9. Michael J. Fox
10. Sidney Poitier

Are PLATO, ARISTOTLE, and SOCRATES one and THE same PERSON?
(1950)

*P*lato, Aristotle, and Socrates are not the same person. They are considered to be the "Big Three" of the ancient Greek philosophers. Socrates was a philosopher in ancient Athens who was accused and convicted of corrupting the youth. His punishment was death. Plato was a rich aristocrat who became an enthusiastic and talented student of Socrates. He wrote famous dialogues featuring Socrates verbally grappling with opponents. In turn, Aristotle became Plato's best student. Aristotle became the tutor of Alexander the Great and was probably the highest paid philosopher in history. The World Book Online Reference Center has additional information for budding philosophy enthusiasts.

HAS A COW UPPER TEETH?
(N.D.)

Cows do not have upper incisors; instead there's what's known as a "dental pad." *Storey's Guide to Raising Beef Cattle*, 3rd ed., by Heather Smith Thomas describes this as, "a patch of tough skin covering their gums. Grass and other forage is cut off with the lower teeth biting against the dental pad or with tongue wrapping around the grass and a swing of the head." It's not in the book, but we should mention that this is the real reason why when you see photographs of cows, they are never smiling. It's not, contrary to popular belief, because cows object to photographers' use of the word "cheese."

DO YOU HAVE ANY INSPIRATIONAL MATERIAL ON GRASS AND LAWNS?
(1955)

*W*ell, you could start with Whitman's American masterpiece *Leaves of Grass* while you wait for *The Lawn Bible* to arrive. *The American Lawn* by Georges Teyssot (Princeton Architectural Press, 1999) examines the place of the lawn in America's cultural landscape, exploring it through historical, artistic, literary, and political contexts and "situating it on the boundary between utopian ideal and dystopian nightmare." For practical advice, perhaps *The Lawn Bible* by David Mellor (Hachette Books, 2003) offers some inspiration on how to cultivate and maintain a lawn like a master groundskeeper.

CAN YOU TELL ME WHO PAINTED THE PAINTING "WHISTLER'S MOTHER"?
(1965)

James Abbott McNeill Whistler (1834–1903) painted *Arrangement in Grey and Black No.1* in 1871. The subject is the artist's mother, Anna McNeill Whistler, though it is rumored that Whistler's beautiful young neighbor Helena Lindgren would sit in his mother's place when she grew tired. The painting become known as *Whistler's Mother* perhaps after it was listed for the 1872 exhibition at the Royal Academy of Art in London: *Arrangement in Grey and Black: Portrait of the Painter's Mother*. The painting is currently part of the French state collection at the Musée d'Orsay in Paris (musee-orsay.fr).

Can you tell me who painted the painting "Whistler's Mother"?

WHAT LASSITUDE IS NYC ON?
(1959)

*A*ccording to LatLong.net, NYC is latitude: 40.730610. NYC is also sometimes known to be in a state of "lassitude," but not often. Merriam-Webster.com defines lassitude as "a condition of weariness or debility: fatigue."

WHAT IS THE POPULARITY OF
ELMWOOD, LONG ISLAND?
(1959)

*E*lwood" (NOT Elmwood), Long Island, is a
census-designated place in Suffolk County,
New York, and an unincorporated village within
the town of Huntington, New York (hunting-
tonny.gov). *Population* for Elwood in the 2010
census was 11,177. This statistic might also attest
to its popularity.

WHAT IS THE NUTRITIONAL VALUE
OF HUMAN FLESH?
(1958)

*H*annibal Lecter would truly have to be a serial killer—if he intended to live solely from human flesh. The human body is edible and there have been documented instances of human cannibalism for thousands of years and across many cultures. And human flesh has been used as one form of nutrition from Paleolithic times to those desperate for food in twentieth-century concentration camps and among survivors of disasters in remote areas.

However, according to one recent study of "nutritional human cannibalism" during the Paleolithic (when there was no evidence cannibalism was practiced for a spiritual or ritual purpose) the human body is not an optimal resource in terms of the sheer number of calories that it provides when compared to other sources of meat. The study estimates that, if consumed, a human body would provide an average of 125,000 to 144,000 calories. This means that the meat on one human's body could have provided a group of twenty-five modern adult males with enough calories to survive for only about half a day. In contrast, that same tribe during Paleolithic times could have feasted on a mammoth that, with 3.6 million calories, would have provided enough sustenance for sixty days. Even a steppe bison would offer 612,000 calories, which is enough for ten days of nourishment.

The study suggests that because humans offered such a comparatively low amount of calories that some examples of Paleolithic cannibalism that had been interpreted as "nutritional" may have occurred for social or cultural reasons.

ISN'T THERE SOMEBODY WHO CAN ANSWER MY QUESTIONS WITHOUT HAVING TO LOOK IN A BOOK? (1960)

*T*he Oracle! Dictionaries define the Oracle of Delphi in Greek mythology as the place (Apollo's Temple) where a priestess supposedly delivered messages from Apollo to those who sought advice. Like this answer may seem, the messages were usually obscure or ambiguous. In reality, no—there is not a person such as you seek. Here at the NYPL, we value books, but we'll let Patti Smith further answer this question with her own words as she accepted the National Book Award: "I've always loved books, all my life . . . there's nothing more beautiful than the book, the paper, the font, the cloth, there is nothing in our material world more beautiful than the book." Any other questions?

WHAT WAS THE EFFECT OF THE ROMAN INVASION ON ENGLISH-LANGUAGE LITERATURE? (1961)

*T*he effect of the Roman invasion on English literature was vast and extends from Shakespeare to Harry Potter, as it introduced Latin as well as classical literature, history, cultural norms, and vocabulary to English literature. Shakespeare's allusions and imaginary expeditions to ancient Rome are extensive. *Titus Andronicus, Julius Caesar, Coriolanus,* and sections of *Antony and Cleopatra* are often referred to as Shakespeare's "Roman plays" and references to Roman culture are peppered throughout his other works. Roman influence is found in an enormous amount of other English literature that would certainly include the works of John Milton, Samuel Johnson, Elizabeth Barrett Browning, James Joyce, P. G. Wodehouse, and even J. K. Rowling's Harry Potter novels.

Is there a book on how-to-build
with popsicle sticks?

IS THERE A BOOK ON HOW-TO-BUILD WITH POPSICLE STICKS? (1967)

We don't have a specific title for arts and crafts solely using popsicle sticks but you might want to browse through the general arts and crafts section of the library: Dewey number 745.

IN 1962, WHAT WAS THE PIGEON POPULATION OF NEW YORK COMPARED WITH THE SPARROW POPULATION IN 2018?

*T*he 1959 book *A Natural History of New York City* by John Kieran offers as close an estimate as we can find for the year 1962. Kieran writes, "The Common Pigeon or Rock Dove (*Columba livia*), a hardy bird and steady breeder through all months of the year, is present in numbers that some persons consider appalling. Estimates of the pigeon population vary from 250,000 to 350,000 or more but these are mere guesses. Nobody has bothered to take a citywide census of these birds that, strangely enough, are most abundant on the pavement of the crowded sections of the city and live entirely on handouts from humans. Fifty years ago the Pigeons were out-numbered by the House Sparrow (*Passer domesticus*), but the automobiles that drove the horses off the city streets took the food out of the mouths of the House Sparrows . . . ."

Estimates of the current pigeon population in the five boroughs is one million. The book *Field Guide to the Neighborhood Birds of New York City* by Leslie Day and Don Riepe states that *Passer domesticus,* "is the most commonly seen bird throughout the five boroughs and lives here year round."

For expert help, be sure to contact Audubon New York, "the voice for birds in New York State."

Incidentally neither bird is native to North America.

I AM FROM WILMINGTON, NORTH CAROLINA, AND MY DADDY OWNS THE SECOND OLDEST LIGHTHOUSE IN THE COUNTRY. WHERE CAN I SELL IT?
(1961)

NYPL does have resources to help you find licensed real estate agents, and find places where you can directly sell real property. It may be worthwhile contacting the United States Lighthouse Society, which is a nonprofit organization working, ". . . to educate, inform, and entertain those who are interested in lighthouses, past and present."

WHAT IS THE GESTATION PERIOD FOR HUMAN BEINGS IN DAYS?
(1962)

*I*t is often difficult to say when the stork will arrive. Gestation is neither logical nor predictable. An unborn baby spends approximately 259 days, or thirty-seven weeks, in the woman's uterus. The average length of pregnancy, or gestation, is actually calculated as "280 days" because the average length of pregnancy is counted from the first day of the woman's last period, not the date of conception that generally occurs about two weeks later followed by five to seven days before it settles in the uterus. This is also the "forty weeks" that most resources refer to and forty weeks are ten lunar months. Most people, however, think in terms of the Gregorian calendar. Therefore, "nine months" is also given as a standard period of human gestation.

When the woman does not go into labor on

her due date, the medical provider has to explain that the gestation period is actually a period of time and not an exact date. It is the time frame of two weeks before the due date or two weeks after it. So any pregnancy between thirty-eight and forty-two weeks is considered to be normal. For all these reasons, only about 4 percent of women actually give birth on their due date while approximately 70 percent give birth within ten days of their due date.

There are many online pregnancy calculators. A very rough and simple method is to add seven days to the first day of the last period, then add nine months. Methods to obtain a more accurate estimate for the length of gestation include: an ultrasound examination (especially when performed between six and twelve weeks), size of uterus as gauged by a medical professional during an examination, and a very approximate guide is the time fetal movements are first felt.

CAN THE NYPL RECOMMEND A GOOD FORGER? (A WOMAN ASKED, IN PERSON, IN 1963)

While NYPL would not recommend anyone who produces fraudulent copies, you can find information about famous forgers in our collections and online. On Artsy.net, there is a brief history of art forgery that includes a story about Michelangelo, who, in 1496, sculpted a sleeping cupid, then buried it to make it appear older. When the cardinal who bought the work discovered the sculpture was not antique, he demanded a refund from the dealer, but allowed Michelangelo to keep his portion of the proceeds because he was so impressed with the work. So perhaps we might recommend Michelangelo.

DO ANY ANIMALS EXPECTORATE THEIR YOUNG? (1965)

*T*he 2003 book *Aquarium Fish Breeding* by Jay F. Hemdal describes the only relevant animals that we've found: "Mouthbrooders find that a safe place to incubate their eggs is in the mouth cavity of one of the parent fish, often the female. This behavior is sometimes incorrectly referred to as mouthbreeding, but as the fish are only holding (or brooding). . . . The eggs are well protected from predators while in the parent's mouth, but the energy cost to the adult is very high since they cannot feed at all during the time they are brooding their young." When the eggs hatch the fry leave the parent's mouth and become free swimming—and the mom or dad fish can eat again!

Among the species we found that are mouthbrooders are Tanganyika cichlids, Banggai cardinalfish, hardhead sea catfish, pearly jawfish, and the peppermint pikehead.

CAN YOU PLEASE TELL ME WHAT
"HIGHER WATER" MEANS? I THINK
IT HAD SOMETHING TO DO WITH
THE EARLY AMERICAN INDIANS.
(1965)

*H*igher Water" doesn't ring a bell, sorry. Could you perhaps be asking about Hiawatha? Hiawatha (also known as hī-ə-ˈwȯ-thə, ˌhē-ə-, -ˈwä- in the Onondaga language) was a precolonial Native American leader and cofounder of the Iroquois Confederacy. The name means (approximately) "he who combs." *The Song of Hiawatha* is a famed 1855 poem by Henry Wadsworth Longfellow, and has been notably parodied in James Warner Ward's *The Song of Higher-Water*. If it's not Hiawatha you're looking for, could you perhaps be asking about "root" or "birch" beer, aka Hires water?

WHERE IN NEW YORK CAN I GET AN ORIGINAL GOLD NUGGET?
(1966)

*A*las, if anyone has found gold in New York State recently they are keeping that news to themselves. We could not find a single article about gold being found in the state in the New York State Newspaper database in the past couple of years. If you're interested in trying your luck you might want to join the Gold Prospectors Association of America. And if you do find some gold be sure to familiarize yourself with the New York Consolidated Laws, Public Lands Law— PBL § 82. Notice of discovery; filing; fee; bounty to discover; royalty to state.

WHO BUILT THE ENGLISH CHANNEL?
(1966)

*W*hile some might say that Mother Nature built the English Channel, it all comes down to melting ice at the end of the Ice Age. Many geologists believe that a low-lying plain once connected what is now known as England and France. Approximately 7,000 years ago, large amounts of ice melted nearby and the resulting water raised the level of the sea, flooding the low-lying plain and creating the English Channel (World Book Online Reference Center).

WHO WAS THE REAL DRACULA?
(1972)

*F*or an answer to this question look no further than Bram Stoker's Notes and Outlines for *Dracula* that are held in the Rosenbach Museum and Library in Philadelphia. In her book *Dracula: Sense and Nonsense,* Elizabeth Miller writes that Stoker got the idea for the name Dracula from the book *An Account of the Principalities of Wallachia and Maldovia* by William Wilkinson that the author borrowed from the Whitby Public Library. In his notes he wrote "Dracula in the Wallachian language means devil."

Who was the real Dracula?

COULD YOU GIVE ME A RUNDOWN ON KIPLING, THE INDIANA [SIC] POET WHO WROTE "BAA, BAA, BLACK SHEEP"? (1967)

While the state of Indiana might like to claim Joseph Rudyard Kipling as one of its own, the British are likely to have strong opinions on the matter. Kipling, the British poet/author, was born in Bombay (now Mumbai), India, in 1865. Some of his most famous stories included Indian characters and/or settings. According to the Literature Resource Center and the World Book Online Reference Center, "Baa, Baa, Black Sheep" was the title that Kipling used for a semi-autobiographical short story that he published in 1888.

CAN YOU GIVE ME THE STRUCTURAL DEFICIENCIES OF "BEOWULF"? (N.D.)

*H*ere is one of the ways you can explore *Beowulf*: "The Style and Structure of Beowulf" by Joan Blomfield (*Review of English Studies*, vol. os-14, issue 56, October 1, 1938, pp. 396–403).

WHAT IS THE NATURAL ENEMY
OF A DUCK? (1967)

*A*lmost any two- or four-footed predator will eat a duck if it has the chance. This includes unleashed New York City canines. The most common enemies of the duck are: foxes, coyotes, weasels, and small bears. Eagles, hawks, owls, crows, raccoons, skunks, snakes, snapping turtles, and mink should not, however, be overlooked. According to the "Mallard" entry in the Wildlife Directory (University of Illinois Extension), 50 percent of mallard ducks do not survive their first year of life. One can only hope that ducks can outfox their natural enemies, including humans and hunters.

WAS CARRIE NATION THE HEROINE
OF THE BOOK *SISTER CARRIE?*
(1964)

*W*hile Carrie A. Nation was not the protagonist of Theodore Dreiser's classic novel, the famous hatchet-wielding teetotaler likely would have been disdainful of Sister Carrie (aka Caroline Meeber) due to Ms. Nation's hostility toward tobacco, foreign foods, corsets, skirts of improper length, and any general lack of decorum. Interestingly, the original manuscript of *Sister Carrie* (published in 1900) is in the collection of The New York Public Library.

Is there a full moon
every night in Acapulco?

IS THERE A FULL MOON EVERY NIGHT IN ACAPULCO? (1961)

*W*ouldn't that be nice? But as romantic a spot as Acapulco was in 1961, when this question was posed—or as romantic as it still may be—the moon is only full there once a month, as it is in every other spot on the globe. No matter how many margaritas you drink that may help it appear otherwise!

The Almanac, as well as https://www.time anddate.com/moon/phases/mexico/acapulco, can help you decide when to go and what moon you will experience when you are there.

WHEN WAS THE BATTLE OF
CROESUS?
(1967)

*C*roesus was said to be the wealthiest man in the ancient world and is best remembered for the battle of Sardis in c. 546 BC. Croesus lost this battle to Cyrus the Great of Persia. According to Herodotus—the Greek historian known as "the father of history" but also as the "father of lies" "in part for inserting mythology into his accounts"—before setting out Croesus consulted with the Oracle of Delphi, who informed Croesus that if he attacked the Persians: "he would destroy a great empire."

After an initial indecisive clash, as it was almost winter, Croesus decided to return home. At that moment, Cyrus's army appeared on the plain of Sardis. Cyrus ordered his cavalry to unload their pack camels and mount them to face the cavalry of Croesus mounted on horses. Cyrus did this because horses are afraid of camels and cannot endure to see or smell them. Croesus and his army were defeated and Croesus was captured and afterward may have been put to death. So Croesus did destroy a great empire—but it was his own.

WHY DO 18TH-CENTURY ENGLISH PAINTINGS HAVE SO MANY SQUIRRELS IN THEM, AND HOW DID THEY TAME THEM SO THAT THEY WOULDN'T BITE THE PAINTER?
(1976)

*F*or upper-class families of the 1700s, squirrels were very popular pets. Children truly enjoyed these fluffy devil-may-care rodents so naturally they made their way into portraits and paintings of the time. In most cases, however, the painter would use a reference from books on nature and animals rather than live squirrels, thus bypassing the need to tame them to sit still and pose!

Why do 18th-century English paintings have so many squirrels in them, and how did they tame them so they wouldn't bite the painter?

IS THERE A LIST OF MOVIE STARS
WITH PIERCED EARS?
(1968)

*N*ot that we are aware of. Actually, online there are a few guides to piercing that feature celebrities, but none are specifically about pierced ears. *Glamour* magazine's website posted a list of "The best celebrity piercings—ever!" on October 25, 2017, in case you are interested in descriptions of "Rihanna's numerous earrings" or Paris Jackson's oversized earrings (and nose ring).

DO YOU HAVE A BOOK ABOUT REINCARNATION THAT IS ILLUSTRATED?
(1967)

*T*he Library carries many books on this topic but not a lot with illustrations. One title that came up in our search is a children's book, *The Mysteries of Reincarnation,* by Daniel Cohen.

WHERE CAN I FIND YOUR DEPARTMENT WHICH HAS MATERIAL ON THE ACRYLIC ALPHABET? (1973)

You could try https://www.nailstyle.com /posts/Nail-Tips-Guide-The-ABCs-Of -Nails-1126 or do you perhaps mean the Cyrillic alphabet? In which case . . . look under Dewey number 491.

IS THERE A LIST OF MUSEUMS THAT
MIGHT BE INTERESTED IN BUYING
A SHRUNKEN HEAD THAT HAS BEEN IN
MY FAMILY FOR YEARS? IT'S THE HEAD
OF A WHITE MAN WHO MAY HAVE COME
FROM THE UPPER AMAZON OR ECUADOR.
(1974)

*W*e did not find a list of museums that currently collect shrunken heads (though they can be found at many museums with major collections in ethnography and anthropology). Shrunken heads, also known as *tsantsa* or *tzantza*, come from the Jivaro Indians of Ecuador and Peru. Authentic tsantsa are rare. The book *1001 Curious Things: Ye Olde Curiosity Shop and Native American Art* by Kate C. Duncan (University of Washington Press, 2000), states that "It has been estimated that about 80 percent of the tsantsas in private and museum hands are fraudulent." The article "Shrunken head (tsantsa): a complete forensic analysis procedure" by Phillippe Charlier, et al. (*Forensic Science International*, Oct. 10, 2012) offers a guide to test authenticity.

WHAT COUNTRY HAS THE HIGHEST NUMBER OF HONORABLE WOMEN? (N.D.)

*T*he answer depends, of course, on how you define "honorable." Women who are referred to as "Honorable" in the United States (ambassadors, judges, and various public officials) in other countries might be called "Her Excellency" instead. For the looser definition of the term, meaning woman of high morals, it would be impossible to say!

Does anyone have a copyright on the Bible?

DOES ANYONE HAVE A COPYRIGHT ON THE BIBLE? (1979)

*T*he answer to that question depends on which version you're talking about. Rights in *The Authorized Version of the Bible* (King James Bible) in the United Kingdom are vested in the Crown and administered by the Crown's patentee, Cambridge University Press. The reproduction by any means of the text of the King James Version is permitted to a maximum of five hundred (500) verses for liturgical and noncommercial educational use, provided that the verses quoted neither amount to a complete book of the Bible nor represent 25 percent or more of the total text of the work in which they are quoted, subject to the following acknowledgment being included: Scripture quotations from The Authorized (King James) Version. Rights in the Authorized Version in the United Kingdom are vested in the Crown. Reproduced by permission of the Crown's patentee, Cambridge University Press.

WAS THE FETUS OF THE SEAL EVER USED IN MAKING FUR COATS?
(N.D.)

*A*n April 1899 edition of the *Journal of Zoophily* states that a Professor Gambier Bolton testified seeing "pregnant seals ripped open [and] the fetus torn away . . . to make the extra soft and delicate fetal sealskin, prized even more highly than the fetal Llama and Astrakan skin (all by the way, obtained in the same manner). . . ." There is no mention of how the pelts are to be used.

HOW DO YOU GROW HAIR ON YOUR CHEST? (N.D.)

*I*f your life is not "harried" enough, you might be entertained by this nonacademic source while you sip on your whiskey and Tabasco drink: The artofmanliness.com's posting (https://www .artofmanliness.com/articles/it-will-put-hair -chest/) says that black coffee, Tabasco sauce, bread crust, hard work, Wheaties, whiskey, spinach, horseradish sauce, Worcestershire sauce, and buttermilk would supposedly do the trick. But even they agree that testosterone and genetics are what really makes it happen.

IF THE EMPIRE STATE BUILDING IS THE HIGHEST BUILDING IN THE WORLD, WHAT IS THE SMALLEST? (N.D.)

*T*here is no date on this question, but we assume that it was asked before 1970 when the North Tower of the World Trade Center became the tallest building in the world. At present, the tallest building in the world is the 2,717 foot tall Burj Khalifa in Dubai.

The Newby-McMahon Building, located in Wichita Falls, Texas, is commonly known as the world's smallest skyscraper—at forty feet tall. You can find out more about the building and the swindler who built it on the Atlas Obscura website.

Can a Bubble Be Described as "Billowy"? (n.d.)

Merriam-Webster defines "billowy" as like a great surge of water, or a rolling mass. And the *Oxford English Dictionary* defines its verb form "billow" as: "to fill with air and swell outwards," which a bubble definitely might be doing. The *OED* also notes that it started to be used in the mid-sixteenth century, evolving from the Old Norse word *bylgja*.

HOW DOES A BEET REPRODUCE ITSELF? (N.D.)

*B*irds do it, bees do it—but beets do it somewhat differently.

The flower is the reproductive structure of the beet plant and it includes both the stamen that produces pollen grains that contains sperm cells that fertilize the egg cell inside the embryo sac in the ovary that is also located in the flower. Once the pollen is transferred—by wind in a natural setting—fertilization has occurred and the zygote grows into an embryo and the ovary forms the seed coat. The beet seed contains an embryo and perisperm for the embryo to feed on.

IS A "HYDRAULIC RAM" A WATER GOAT? (N.D.)

While sounding like a particularly salacious dance move from the 1970s, the "hydraulic ram" is actually neither dance, nor goat, but an apparatus that moves water (hydro being a prefix meaning water) from one place to another.

What do you feed
a salamander?

WHAT DO YOU FEED A
SALAMANDER?
(1983)

Salamanders are carnivores and they range in size. They can be as small as one inch with the largest reaching up to six feet. No worries, despite how big some species can get, humans are never on the menu! Large salamanders prefer fish, crayfish, aquatic insects, frogs, snakes, and small mammals like mice. Smaller to medium salamanders prefer worms and other invertebrates, slugs, mollusks, spiders, and snails. You can find more books on the care and feeding of salamanders under the Dewey number 597.85.

HOW MANY ACRES ARE THERE IN A MILE? (N.D.)

*S*ince an acre is a measure of area and a mile a measure of length—perchance you mean a square mile (which would then become a measure of area)? In any case, the original definition of acre indicated the amount of land it would take two oxen to till in one calendar day. So depending on the strength, endurance, and employee benefits of your particular oxen-twosome, this definition is variable.

DO YOU HAVE BOOKS ABOUT EMBALMING? (N.D.)

*W*e have several! Here are just a few of the titles we own:

Earthly Remains: The History and Science of Preserved Human Bodies by Andrew Chamberlain (New York: Oxford University Press, 2001).

Embalming and Its Medical and Legal Aspects (New York, 1931).

Embalming Fluids: Their Historical Development and Formulation, from the Standpoint of the Chemical Aspect of the Scientific Art of Preserving Human Remains by Simon Mendelsohn (New York: Chemical Publishing Co, 1940).

Embalming: History, Theory and Practice by Robert G. Mayer (2nd ed., Stamford, Conn: Appleton & Lange, 1996).

Hygiene and Sanitary Science: A Practical Guide

for Embalmers and Sanitarians by Albert John Nunnamaker (Cincinnati, Ohio: The Embalming Book Company, 1923).

Modern Mummies: The Preservation of the Human Body in the Twentieth Century by Christine Quigley (Jefferson, NC: McFarland & Co., 1998).

Morgue Guide: A Manual of Embalming by Samuel Henry (Atlanta: 1954).

IS A BLACK WIDOW SPIDER MORE HARMFUL DEAD OR ALIVE? (N.D.)

*T*he venom of the black widow spider can cause nausea, severe muscle pain, and paralysis of the diaphragm among other symptoms. Despite this, death is a rare occurrence. Venom is defined by the *Oxford English Dictionary* as "the poisonous fluid normally secreted by certain snakes and other animals and used by them in attacking other living creatures." Therefore if the black widow is dead they cannot attack, which means they are more harmful alive. Even if you were to gasp and consume the spider, the venom would not affect you because it must be injected into the bloodstream via a bite to be effective.

Is there a list of buildings
that were designed and built in
the shapes of fruits or vegetables?

IS THERE A LIST OF BUILDINGS THAT WERE DESIGNED AND BUILT IN THE SHAPES OF FRUITS OR VEGETABLES?
(1983)

While there are numerous books on the topic of novelty architecture (including "mimetic" buildings), such as Jim Heimann's 2001 *California Crazy and Beyond: Roadside Vernacular Architecture* and *The Colossus of Roads: Myth and Symbol along the American Highway* by Karal Ann Marling, we found no source that lists buildings in the shapes of fruits or vegetables. Some of the fruit-and-vegetable-shaped structures we did find in some of the books in our collections include Castroville, California's, giant artichoke stand, the Ear of Corn Rest Area, in Olivia, Minnesota, and Tokyo, Japan's, Sanrio Strawberry House. Do doughnuts count as a vegetable?

IS IT proper to wear a veil at nighttime? (n.d.)

According to the *Berg Encyclopedia of World Dress and Fashion,* there are no known restrictions on donning a veil at any time of day. Rather, the practice of veiling is usually associated with women and sacred objects, though in some cultures it is men rather than women who are expected to wear a veil. Besides its enduring religious significance, veiling continues to play a role in some modern secular contexts, most notably wedding customs.

Today, there is much discussion and interest in a specific type of veil called a "hijab." Looking into the function of this specific veil may give us a deeper answer to the question. Preferred by modern Muslim women, a hijab is a headscarf worn over the head and hair but leaving the face uncovered regardless of time of day. "Hijab" comes from the Arabic word meaning "cover" or "curtain," "barrier" or "partition." A broader meaning would be "modesty, morality, privacy." Hijab is not mandated for women in front of their male relatives or other Muslim women, but rather for men they may, theoretically, marry. "Hijab, in the sense of veiling, can also be achieved by hanging a curtain or placing a screen between women and men to allow them to speak to each other without changing dress. This was more common in the early days of Islam, for the wives of the Prophet Muhammad." BBC.co.uk/religion/islam/beliefs.

WHEN WEST POINT CADETS
THROW THEIR HATS IN THE AIR AT
GRADUATION, DO THEY EVER GET
THEM BACK? (N.D.)

At West Point at the immortal words: "You are dismissed" the cadets fling their hats into the air. West Point rules permit children under the age of ten to recover the caps. West Point cadets probably could recover their hats—if they really wanted to. Most cadets traditionally write their names and possibly some words of inspiration or encouragement inside their hat and may still leave a small amount of money that reflects their graduation year. In any case, there is nothing wrong with the graduates tossing away a part of their uniform. It's no longer their proper uniform anyway. They've just been promoted!

WHAT IS THE more affectionate
ending for a letter –
"affectionately yours" or
"yours as ever"? (n.d.)

According to EmilyPost.com, "as ever" is useful in closing a letter to someone with whom you may not be close or haven't seen for some time. For friendly, intimate closings, "Affectionately" is frequently used.

WHO SAID "NEW PRESBYTER IS BUT OLD PRIEST WRIT LARGE"? (N.D.)

John Milton wrote these lines in a 1646 poem entitled: "On the New Forcers of Conscience under the Long Parliament." It was written during the English Civil War and reflects Milton's Puritan view that the Long Parliament at that time was attempting to force the English church into closer conformity with the Church of Scotland that was governed by a system of elected "presbyters" and this offered insufficient liberty of conscience to Puritan congregations and worshipers. To Milton, it was not enough to replace Church of England priests and bishops with presbyters. The English Civil War and its many religious disputes played a role in the provisions of the U.S. Constitution that guarantee the free exercise of religion.

WHere can I rent a GUILLOTine?
(n.d.)

*R*enting a guillotine is very possible, as long as you don't want a real one. Believe it or not there are real guillotines still in existence but they are held by private collectors and museums. As reported by NPR, a 150-year-old replica was recently sold at an auction in France to a French industrialist. Okay, now that we've established real guillotines are not a possibility; for entertainment purposes, there are prop houses that rent full-size models of the type of guillotine used for execution. However, if you're hoping to rent a guillotine to play Robespierre for real, you're out of luck. On the other hand, there are different sorts of guillotine-like devices used for vari-

Where can I rent
a guillotine?

ous purposes. These include industrial guillotines for trimming paper, metal, meats, and other food products, which can be rented or leased via industrial suppliers (which can be researched at our Science, Industry and Business Library).

DO YOU HAVE ANY BOOKS ON "HUMAN BEINGS"? (N.D.)

Yes, we have more books on "human beings" than one can read in a lifetime. You may want to start at the beginning with something like *The Human Past: World Prehistory and the Development of Human Societies* edited by Chris Scarre or *Close Encounters with Humankind: a Paleoanthropologist Investigates our Evolving Species* by Sang-Hee Lee and Shin-Young Yoon. For something lighter and more visual, try *Humans of New York: Stories* by Brandon Stanton. Investing in some reading glasses might be a good idea.

ACKNOWLEDGMENTS

With thanks to the contributors from The New York Public Library:

Anne Barreca,
Library Manager, Battery Park City

Matthew Boylan,
Senior Librarian, AskNYPL Virtual Reference

Rosa Caballero-Li,
AskNYPL Manager

Frank Collerius,
Library Manager, Jefferson Market

Sean Ferguson, Library Manager, Chatham Square

Louise Lareau,
Managing Librarian, Stephen A. Schwarzman Building, Children's Center

Bernard van Maarseveen,
Assistant Manager, AskNYPL Virtual Reference

Chasity Moreno,
Senior Librarian, AskNYPL Virtual Reference

Jill Rothstein,
Chief Librarian, Andrew Heiskell Library

Carrie Welch,
Chief External Relations Officer

Matthew Kirby,
Executive Assistant

NOTES

Did Abraham Lincoln
go to Harvard?

Bartelt, William E. *There I Grew Up: Remember-
ing Abraham Lincoln's Indiana Youth* (Indianapo-
lis, IN: Indiana Historical Society Press, 2008)
p. 118.; Donald, David Herbert. *Lincoln* (New
York: Simon & Schuster, 1995), pp. 30–32.; Peter-
son, Merrill D. *Lincoln in American Memory* (New
York and Oxford: Oxford University Press, 1994),
pp. 110–12.

What is the eye color of a silver fox?

https://www.worldatlas.com/articles/silver-fox-facts
-animals-of-north-america.html, https://livingwith
foxes.weebly.com/red-fox-color-mutations.html,
and as to the gray fox: http://tracker.cci.fsu.edu
/greyfox/about/who/.

What is the nutritional value of human flesh?

Citations: St. Fleur, Nicholas. "Ancient Cannibals
Didn't Eat Just for the Calories, Study Suggests,"
New York Times (April 6, 2017): https://www
.nytimes.com/2017/04/06/science/cannibalism
-human-body-calories.html; Engelhaupt, Erica.
"Cannibalism Study Finds People Are Not That
Nutritious," *National Geographic* (April 2017):
https://news.nationalgeographic.com/2017/04

/human-cannibalism-nutrition-archaeology
-science/; Lindenbaum, Shirley. "Thinking About
Cannibalism," *Annual Review of Anthropology* 33
(2004), pp. 475–98: https://search-proquest-com
.i.ezproxy.nypl.org/pqrl/docview/199817315
/D667B44542BC4310PQ/11?accountid=35635.

What was the effect of the Roman
invasion on English-language literature?

John Milton use of classical models: "Milton's
Use of Classical Mythology in *Paradise Lost*," by
Jonathan H. Collett, *PMLA*, vol. 85, no. 1 (Jan.,
1970), pp. 88–96:

https://www.jstor.org/stable/1261434?seq=1#page
_scan_tab_contents.

Samuel Johnson—Latin poems and influence on
Latin on his poems:

https://www.poetryfoundation.org/poets/samuel
-johnson.

https://andromeda.rutgers.edu/~jlynch/Johnson
/Guide/poems.html.

Elizabeth Barrett Browning—Latin:

https://www.poetryfoundation.org/poets
/elizabeth-barrett-browning.

Virgil—influence on James Joyce:

https://www.jstor.org/stable/40388971?seq
=1#page_scan_tab_contents.

Roman influence on T. S. Elliot, P. G. Wodehouse, and J. K. Rowling:

https://penandthepad.com/effect-did-romans
-english-literature-8468363.html.

Victoria, Australia, government website: https://
www.betterhealth.vic.gov.au/health/healthyliving
/baby-due-date.

https://www.quora.com/Why-do-people-say-a
-pregnancy-is-nine-months-when-it-is-actually
-40-weeks. https://www.sciencedaily.com/releases
/2013/08/130806203327.htm.

https://www.britannica.com/event/Siege-of
-Sardis-546-BCE.

http://www.livius.org/articles/person/croesus/.

https://www.britannica.com/biography/Croesus.

https://www.jstor.org/stable/10.1086/505670?seq
=1#page_scan_tab_contents, pp. 46–48.

How does the beet reproduce itself?

Email of Philp V. Ammirato [Professor Emeritus of Biological Sciences, Barnard College] to Matthew J. Boylan dated August 29, 2018: "Your statement re perisperm is correct. The embryo in the seed develops when the sperm cell carried by the pollen grain fuses with the egg cell inside the embryo sac in the ovary to form the zygote. The zygote grows into the embryo and the ovary forms the seed coat. The embryo is helped along the way in most flowering plants by the special tissue, the endosperm. . . . In a small number of plants, beet being one of them, there is no endosperm. Its place in helping the developing embryo is taken by the perisperm."

https://www.amnh.org/learn/biodiversity_counts/ident_help/Parts_Plants/parts_of_flower.htm.

Biology Discussion—"Beetroot: Origin, Production and Breeding Methods—India," chapter 3, "Botany of Beetroot":

http://www.biologydiscussion.com/vegetable-breeding/beetroot-origin-production-and-breeding-methods-india/68475.

Canadian Food Inspection Agency—B1 "General Description" of related sugar beet:

http://www.inspection.gc.ca/plants/plants-with-novel-traits/applicants/directive-94-08/biology-documents/beta-vulgaris-l-/eng/1330725373948/1330725437349#b1.

Dartmouth College—for poem text:

https://www.dartmouth.edu/~milton/reading
_room/conscience/text.shtml.

Explanation of poem: University of Wisconsin:

https://faculty.history.wisc.edu/sommerville/367
/Milton.html.

On the Westminster Assembly appointed by the
Long Parliament and Presbyterianism:

https://en.wikipedia.org/wiki/Westminster
_Assembly.

aBOUT THE NYPL

*T*he New York Public Library is a free provider of education and information for the people of New York and beyond. With ninety-two locations—including research and branch libraries—throughout the Bronx, Manhattan, and Staten Island, the Library offers free materials, computer access, classes, exhibitions, programming and more to everyone from toddlers to scholars, and has seen record numbers of attendance and circulation in recent years. The New York Public Library serves more than 18 million patrons who come through its doors annually and millions more around the globe who use its resources at www.nypl.org. To offer this wide array of free programming, The New York Public Library relies on both public and private funding. Learn more about how to support the Library at nypl.org/support.

ABOUT THE
ILLUSTRATOR

*B*arry Blitt is a cartoonist and illustrator; his work has appeared in countless magazines, newspapers, and books. He was born in Montreal.